A Guide to Sheltering-In-Place

The Prepper's Survival Guide Series

Don't be scared

Don't panic

Shelter-in-Place

Bryan Foster
MS, Chemistry
MS, Management
MBA

aka *Zion Prepper*

ISBN: 1484927451

ISBN -13: 978-1484927458

The Prepper's Survival Guide:

A Guide to Sheltering-In-Place

Contents

About the Author

First and foremost thanks for purchasing The Prepper's Survival Guide: Sheltering-in-Place. It is truly appreciated. My name is Bryan Foster, aka Zion Prepper, and I'm the author of three books: The Prepper's Handbook, The Christian Prepper's Handbook, and The Prepper's Survival Guide: An Introduction to Prepping and a Guide to Fire. I'm a Christian, family man, and US Navy veteran. I'm an extremely dedicated father and husband with the highlight of my life being my family. As the son of a career military veteran, I had the opportunity to move throughout the United States experiencing different cultures and geography. Like my father, I served in the military as an officer in the United States Navy. I was as a chemist and an officer in charge of an auxiliary security force. My formal educational background includes a BS in Forensic Chemistry, MS in Analytical Chemistry, MBA, and MS in Management.

I'm a well-respected author, lecturer, and consultant on the ins and outs of sheltering-in-place as well as prepping. I have been featured in numerous newspaper articles throughout the United States as well as network television, such as the History Channel.

Find me on FACEBOOK @ www.facebook.com/zionprepper, TWITTER @ www.twitter.com/zionprepper, YOUTUBE @www.youtube.com/zionprepper, or EMAIL @ zionprepper@gmail.com

Introduction

[1]To every [thing there is] a season, and a time to every
purpose under the heaven:
[2]A time to be born, and a time to die; a time to plant, and
a time to pluck up [that which is] planted;
[3]A time to kill, and a time to heal; a time to break down,
and a time to build up;
[4]A time to weep, and a time to laugh; a time to mourn,
and a time to dance;
[5]A time to cast away stones, and a time to gather stones
together; a time to embrace, and a time to refrain from
embracing;
[6]A time to get, and a time to lose; a time to keep, and a
time to cast away;
[7]A time to rend, and a time to sew; a time to keep silence,
and a time to speak;
[8]A time to love, and a time to hate; a time of war, and a
time of peace.
Ecclesiastes Chapter 3

This guide will provide families, groups, or organizations

the information necessary to properly Shelter-in-Place

(SIP). My inspiration for writing this guide is the millions

who had to mandatorily shelter-in-place as a result of the

April 2013 Boston Marathon bombings. My goal is to

support and provide a resource for the millions who have

never sheltered-in-place but one day may be faced with

that necessity. You must be ready to take this action

should it be needed. Throughout this guide, I provide

descriptions and understanding based on practicality and cost. In addition, I offer examples and instructions of when to shelter-in-place. This guide is most practical to those who want to understand sheltering-in-place based on the most common scenario. That scenario is:

- you will shelter-in-place for less than sixteen weeks

- you have neighbors and live in a town or city

- you rely on city or town water, electricity, and sewage

- you understand that in a significant life-altering event stores will quickly run out or not have access to the staples (food, water, bread, etc)

- you're open-minded and understand that you can't predict when you may be required to shelter-in-place

- you want to provide a safe, comfortable environment for yourself, family or group during a significant life-altering event.

It's important to understand that for those who live outside of a town or city the requirements for sheltering-in-place will be somewhat different. In the country you may have access to various water resources such as a well, pond, creek, or river whereas those in the city don't. You may have a large garden while others don't have land for a garden. You get the point. I don't intent for this guide to cover all topics but I do expect to provide you, the reader, with tools necessary to properly shelter-in-place.

Okay, it's time for the legal stuff. As you read through this book, please understand that it is intended for educational purposes only. My statements should not be used as, or in place of, medical advice. I have communicated with experts and conducted extensive research on the topics in this guide, and I have had personal experience with most of the information I present. Nevertheless, I provide this information strictly for your reference and consideration.

Sheltering-in-Place

Sheltering-in-Place is an emergency procedure for individuals, groups, or organizations whereby you seek protection and cover by remaining at your current location, residence, or alternate location. More often than not families will shelter-in-place at their 'primary shelter'. A primary shelter is a residence in which you rely on for protection and comfort. This is most often where you live on a day to day basis such as a house, trailer, apartment, or condominium.

Sheltering-in-place is triggered by natural or man-made events that pose or will pose imminent danger. Individuals, families, or organizations take precautions by:

- remaining at your current location – other than your primary shelter

    o For example, you're on a cruise at sea and told to shelter-in-place. In this example your only option is to shelter-in-place in your cabin.

- You're at a restaurant eating and hear the tornado siren. Once again, you have no choice but to shelter-in-place in the restaurant.

- traveling to your primary shelter from your current location

  - You're eating at a restaurant and realize you need to shelter-in-place because of an impending snow storm. Given you have sufficient time, and it's safe to travel, you would travel from the restaurant to your home where you would shelter-in-place.

- traveling to a pre-determined location other than a primary shelter – i.e. a "bug out" location (aka alternate location).

  - You've been notified that the river two miles from your house has reached flood stage. You realize you're not safe in your primary shelter, your house, so you bug out to a friend's house or other alternate location where you feel safer.

The timing of when to shelter-in-place is based on the event or the availability of information to suggest your life or safety is in danger. Due to the unpredictable nature of when you may have to shelter-in-place, it's vital that you understand all elements of the Survival Triangle©. This will be discussed in detail at a later time.

Mother Nature is often the reason most families shelter-in-place whereas man-made events have forced entire countries to take the same precautions. These significant events are typically known as a Shit-Hits-the-Fan (SHTF) or Significant Life Altering Event (SLAE). It's important to further define a SHTF and SLAE as it directly impacts when, how, and for how long you may have to shelter-in-place.

- Shit Hits the Fan (SHTF): A significant event in which civilization as we know it is forever changed thus requiring individuals, families, or organizations to shelter-in-place for extended periods of time. This acronym describes a dire situation in which individuals, families, or groups must be or become self-reliant. In most situations, individuals using this term assume that humanity is permanently affected and, once again, life as we know it will no longer be the same. Examples of events associated with a SHTF scenario include: martial law, economic collapse, domestic or international terrorism, government collapse, nuclear war, loss of the power grid, and coronal mass ejections. A coronal mass ejection is a release of huge quantities of matter and electromagnetic radiation into space above the sun's surface. These releases disrupt the earth's magnetosphere which can damage or disrupt satellites, space stations, radio waves, and even cause long lasting power outages. More often than not these types of scenarios would require sheltering-in-place for periods of time greater than six months. Words associated with a SHTF include: WROL (without rule of law), TEOTWAWKI (the end of the world as we know it), and BO (bug out).

- Significant Life Altering Event (SLAE): A significant event that takes place in which an individual, group, or organization is affected and must shelter-in-place. Unlike a SHTF situation, a

SLAE does not necessarily have an impact on all of humanity, though it could. In addition, the events of a SLAE can be of personal origins, not necessarily caused by mankind or nature, and could be temporary or permanent dependent on circumstances. Examples of events associated with a SLAE include: death of a family member, loss of a job, snow storm, coronal mass ejection, government collapse, and tornado.

Note: In both a SHTF and SLAE scenario, sheltering-in-place relies on prior planning and stored preparations. The difference between a SHTF and SLAE is who's affected (an individual, family, group, or humanity) and the intensity of the event (localized earthquake, loss of job, martial law, economic collapse, etc.).

Why Shelter-in-Place

The reason to shelter-in-place is simple and straightforward; to maximize survival and minimize actual and potential threats. Sheltering-in-place does and will provide safety and comfort. If you have to shelter-in-place, and you're prepared, you will have peace of mind knowing your shelter and preparations will sustain you and your family for a period of time, while others panic or become concerned about survival.

Understand that sheltering-in-place is a philosophy that maximizes survival in a number of scenarios, including short- and long-term events. Examples of short-term events include temporary loss of power, local chaos, earthquake, tornado, or snow storm. Examples of a long-term event that can prolong sheltering-in-place include the loss of the nation's infrastructure (electricity, water, communication, transportation, fuel, waste disposal, etc.), economic collapse, war, electromagnetic pulse (EMP), solar flares, and domestic/international terrorism to name a few.

When to Shelter-in-Place

It's critical to shelter-in-place anytime you have knowledge or a concern that external events could or will affect the safety of you, your family, group, or organization. This decision should be based on the most reliable information available at the time. There may even be times when you're ordered to shelter-in-place by law enforcement or government officials.

There are two broad categories of events that trigger when you shelter-in-place, natural and man-made events.

Natural events often require that we shelter-in-place but in many cases we are given advanced notice such as the Nor'easter of February 2013:

*"A massive storm packing hurricane-force winds and blizzard conditions **is sweeping through the Northeast**, dumping nearly 2 feet of snow on New England and knocking out power to more than a half a million customers.*

More than 23 inches of snow had fallen in parts of central Connecticut by early Saturday, and more than 21 inches covered Randolph in southeastern Massachusetts" (Lindsay, 2013).

At other times mother nature gives us a warning that a significant life-altering event may occur but doesn't tell us when. Such is the case with avian bird flu, H7N9, which had not been found in humans previously.

*"Two people in China have died and another remains critical after falling ill with a **strain of bird flu not detected before in humans**, the official Chinese news agency Xinhua reported.... A team of experts assigned by the health commission established that the three cases were human infections of H7N9 avian influenza, which has not been found in humans previously, the news agency reported.... The better known H5N1 avian flu virus has infected more than 600 people since 2003, of which 371 have died, according to the WHO"* (Mullen, 2013).

Counter to mother nature are man-made events. Man-made events can occur at any time, are often impossible to predict, and can have a significant effect on mankind.

An example of a man-made SHTF in which an entire city had to shelter-in-place was the domestic terrorist attack at the Boston Marathon in April 2013. As National Public Radio (NPR) explains:

"Local officials have defended the decision to essentially lock down the city of Boston on Friday while law enforcement searched for a suspect in the Boston Marathon bombing.

Residents were told to remain indoors during the hunt for Dzhokhar Tsarnaev, who survived an early morning shootout

17

with police in the suburb of Watertown during which his brother, Tamerlan, was killed.

Massachusetts Gov. Deval Patrick announced the decision to lock down Watertown and the surrounding areas, including Boston, at a dawn news conference Friday.

"We're asking people to shelter-in-place — in other words, to stay indoors with their doors locked and not to open the door for anyone other than a properly identified law enforcement officer," he said.

It is not unusual to lock down schools and other institutions when there are reports of gunfire. And after the Sept. 11, 2001, terrorist attacks, the nation's air traffic was halted and some other sites thought to be potential targets, such as the New York Stock Exchange, were closed. But to shut down a large part of a metropolitan area is another thing, says Frank Cilluffo, director of the Homeland Security Policy Institute at George Washington University.

"In terms of both scale and scope, the shelter-in-place that was enforced was extraordinary, perhaps even unprecedented, but so too were the circumstances," Cilluffo says" (Naylor, 2013).

There was no advanced warning of this attack and as such it was nearly impossible to prevent. The outcome was devastating in that 3 were killed, over 250 injured, and an entire city had to shelter-in-place.

Where to Shelter-in-Place

Where you shelter-in-place is mandated by:

- your current location (which may or may not be your primary shelter)

- distance to your primary shelter if not currently at that location

- distance to a bug out location if your primary shelter is no longer safe

- weather

- magnitude and type of event

- availability of food, water, heat, and protection at your primary shelter or bug out location

- timing of the SHTF or SLAE event (i.e. did it already occur or are you given advanced notice to determine where you will shelter-in-place)

Once again, you have three options: shelter-in-place where you are, travel to your primary shelter and then shelter-in-place (aka "bug-in"), or bug out to a safer alternate location. Bug in, bug out, primary shelter, and bug-out-location are defined as:

- Bug In, aka shelter-in-place: A scenario in which you stay at your current location and rely on existing preparations and resources for sustainability. Typically a bug in location is a primary residence, apartment, trailer, or other long-term housing.

- Bug Out: A scenario in which you have evaluated your surroundings and determined that it's no longer safe to remain at that location because of manmade or natural disasters. You then head or "bug out" to a predetermined location to ensure the safety of yourself, family, or group.

- Bug Out Location: A secondary location, typically within a two-hour drive, that is used to ensure the safety of the individual, family, or group. Bug out locations can include houses, cabins, campers, trailers, vacant land, neighbors, and even underground shelters.

- Primary Shelter: A primary residence in which you rely on for shelter. This is most often where you live on day to day basis such as a house, trailer, apartment, or condominium.

An example of a situation in which you have no choice but to shelter-in-place at your current location is the Carnival Cruise Line fiasco in February and March 2013. As CNN reported:

"That about sums up how people are describing conditions aboard the Carnival Triumph on Tuesday as tugboats slowly drag the stricken cruise ship toward Alabama -- and freedom for its 3,143 passengers.
Some on the ship reported sewage sloshing around in hallways, flooded rooms and trouble getting enough to eat after a fire in the ship's engine room Sunday left it drifting in the Gulf of Mexico. Passengers dragged their mattresses onto the ship's open deck to stay cool and get away from the nasty smells inside.
"The odor is so bad, people are getting sick and they're throwing up everywhere," said Brent Nutt, whose wife is aboard the ship" (Joe Sutton, 2013).

As can easily be deducted, these passengers had no choice but to shelter-in-place and make the best out of a dire situation.

An example of when you are given ample time to leave your current location and head to your primary shelter is, once again, the winter storm of February 2013:

"Blizzard conditions again descended on the midsection of the country Monday, bringing hurricane-force winds to the Texas Panhandle, closing highways in Texas and Oklahoma and putting already snow-covered parts of Kansas on high alert as the day progressed.

National Weather Service officials ***issued blizzard warnings and watches*** *in Kansas and Oklahoma through late Monday. As the storm tracks north and east across West Texas toward Oklahoma, Arkansas, Kansas, and Missouri"* (Blaney, 2013).

In this case there was absolutely no excuse why individuals or families should not have been able to shelter-in-place at their primary shelter as the weather service gave advanced notice of the storm.

An extreme example of when you may want to bug-out to an alternate location that provides additional safety above and beyond that of your primary location is a nuclear event; either local or internationally. Jehtro Mullen of CNN describes one such situation:

> "*The North Koreans need to understand if they attack an American interest or an ally of this country, they're going to pay a heavy price,*" *Graham said on NBC's* "*Meet The Press*" *on Sunday.* "*<u>I could see a major war happening if the North Koreans overplay their hand</u> this time, because the public in South Korea, the United States, and I think the whole region, is fed up with this guy*" (Stableford, 2013).

This is an extreme example but nevertheless can be applied to similar situations such as floods, nuclear power plant meltdown, chemical/biological attack, economic crisis, power grid failure, and many more. The decision to bug out is a personal decision based upon the information at hand, your risk tolerance, and timing.

The Survival Triangle

You effectively shelter-in-place by being PREPARED, PREPARED, AND PREPARED. If you try and prepare to shelter-in-place after a significant life-altering event it's too late. You will have to make do with what you have available. By the time you realize you don't have or are low on critical supplies I can guarantee you that the staples such as milk, bread, sugar, flour, and bottled water will be gone. This is why you prepare in advance with a focus on understanding The Survival Triangle©. The Survival Triangle© models the requirements, balance, and interdependence needed to properly shelter-in-place. Furthermore, each of those elements is supported by experience.

The Survival Triangle© - Courtesy of Zion Prepper aka Bryan Foster

On each corner of the Survival Triangle© is a requirement to safely and properly shelter-in-place:

- Heat (Fire)/Shelter
- Water/Food
- Self-Preservation

The Survival Triangle© provides a balanced approach to sheltering-in-place by indicating the importance of all elements required to shelter-in-place. Should any one element, or corner, be missing, your survival or that of your family or group is in jeopardy. For example, without the food or water elements, it may not matter if you have shelter, heat, or skills in self-preservation. The reason is simple. You will be challenged to remain hydrated and have the protein you need to maintain proper nutrition. Without self-preservation skills you may not be able to mentally function in a significant life-altering event or know how to properly handle a weapon. Let's now *briefly* discuss each element of the Survival Triangle© to better understand their interdependence followed by a detailed description of what to prepare.

Fire (Heat)/Shelter

Without shelter and heat (fire), you won't survive a harsh winter, regardless of food, water, or self-preservation. Shelter keeps you warm in cold weather and dry in the rain. Your shelter also protects your preparations and provides psychological comfort (think: "home sweet home"). Your shelter is a place where you can rest your body while providing protection from threats created by natural and manmade events.

Heat (fire) has a direct impact on many things, including the human body, food supplies, and water stores. The most important aspect of heat is its effect on the human body. The body regulates its temperature (98.6° F) to keep all its systems functioning correctly. The balance between body fluids and warmth is both critical and fragile.

Water/Food

You need water for many reasons, such as to stay hydrated, cook, bathe, brush your teeth, care for animals, and grow plants. In the human body, water helps regulate body temperature (through sweat), protects the nervous system, keeps the skin moist, rids the body of waste, and cushions the joints—a critical component of survival. On a daily basis, humans need to replace approximately two and a half quarts of water. Either drinking water or eating foods high in water content accomplishes this.

Food provides the protein and nutrition necessary to produce energy within the body and sustain life. In addition, food provides nutrients that help keep our bones, hair, nails, and skin strong and flexible. In a SHTF situation, food can even be used to trade or barter for other necessities. Beyond this guide, you can further explore the importance of water and food, from a prepper perspective, in The Prepper's Survival Guide: A Guide to Water and Food.

Self-Preservation

Self-preservation is:

- The preservation of your being from harm, danger, or fear and is an instinctive tendency
- A natural or instinctive tendency to act so as to preserve one's own existence
- Behavior that ensures the survival of an organism; it is universal among living organisms

- Protection of oneself from harm or destruction

Self-preservation can be both a controlled and uncontrolled action and reaction. An uncontrolled action or reaction would be when your body instinctively reacts by removing your hand from a hot stove. Before you can think your body removes the source of pain. Your body, without your input, then begins the healing process. When you have fear, your body releases adrenaline to give you increased strength and a heightened awareness to sight, smell, and hearing. This is an uncontrolled reaction. Other uncontrolled self-preservation reaction or actions include: protection (your natural instinct to protect yourself and family), navigation, psychology of self, and being able to physically defend yourself.

Controlled self-preservation actions start with proper planning. These are actions you control and plan for. As you do advanced planning to shelter-in-place you may decide to purchase weapons and store ammunition for protection. Your reaction is to purchase the weapon(s) and ammunition.

Self-preservation plays an integral role into how you shelter-in-place, and defend your shelter, water, and food from both a physical and mental perspective. It mandates that you know how your body will react in a stressful and unpredictable environment. For example, many Iraq and Afghanistan war veterans are seeking treatment for Post Traumatic Stress Disorder (PTSD). The veterans have been taught to understand the signs of PTSD and when to seek help. Though this may be an extreme example, it demonstrates the need to understand the symptoms of stress as well as how to properly minimize the impact. Sheltering-in-place for extended periods of time, even several days, will create stress. The next time you find yourself in a stressful situation, take an inventory of your physical and mental reactions. Do you shake? Does your heart rate increase? Having this understanding allows you to minimize these stressors and deal with the possibility of having to shelter-in-place for an extended period.

Experience

Experience, as applied to sheltering-in-place and The Survival Triangle©, is composed of two parts: the experience you have and the experience you need. Ideally you will have experience in all aspects within the Survival Triangle©, even as limited as it may be. This is not realistic, so you must realize what your weaknesses are. For example, if you've never shot a gun, you'll find it difficult in a sheltering-in-place situation to protect your shelter or family members; you'll blindly aim and hope for the best. If you don't have experience cooking the food you store, you won't know how to cook it at all, let alone cook it to taste. If you've never learned to repair a shelter or use alternative heat sources, you could be in for some long, cold nights. I have a phrase that I always use: "It was an experience I didn't have, but it was a skill I needed, so I went ahead and did it." You need to always have this mentality.

Energy

Energy is required throughout The Survival Triangle©. When I talk about energy, I do not necessarily mean electricity — although electricity greatly simplifies several components of the triangle. I'm referring to physical and mental energy. Examples of physical energy sources include: wood, propane, batteries, steam, generators, wind, and hydroelectric technology. Mental energy, on the other hand, gives us the drive to endure a SHTF or SLAE while we shelter-in-place. Mental energy gives you confidence when you're feeling scared. It allows you to endure the unknown without going crazy. It allows you to provide counsel or comfort to others whom are sheltering-in-place with you. In order to minimize stress while sheltering-in-place, we need both types of energy.

What to Prepare

Now that you understand The Survival Triangle©, it's time to discuss each element in detail. Let's start with water and water storage.

Water

When you shelter-in-place you need to ensure proper, hydration, health, and nutrition. Remember, the average human body is composed of 65 percent water. To maintain that level, a minimum of two quarts of water is required per person per day. If you live in a hot climate, double that to four quarts of water per person per day. After twenty-four hours without water, dehydration can set in. According to the National Institutes of Health symptoms of dehydration include dry or sticky mouth, an inability to produce tears, little to no urine output, lethargy, and sunken eyes. Without water, the ability to breathe becomes much more difficult. Lung function uses up to one pint of water every day, decreasing the body's moisture level through exhalation.

The typical rule of thumb is that a human can survive three minutes without air, three hours without shelter (i.e. a subzero winter), *three days without water*, and three weeks without food. Before you ever need to shelter-in-remember the rule of 2 + 2 which helps with planning. The rule states when you shelter-in-place you need 2 quarts of water for drinking per day + 2 quarts of water for cooking and hygiene per person per day. However I highly recommend you store one gallon of water per day per person for drinking and two quarts of water per person per day for cooking and hygiene.

Many shelter-in-place scenarios won't cause a panic because running water will be available and most events will not last beyond several days. But what if you had to shelter-in-place and running water was not available?

Here are some storage options:

- bottled water by the gallon or pint
- portable water bladders such as the WaterBob™ or Aqua Pod™.
  - Portable water bladders are made of high density polyethylene. They are portable and can contain up to 100 gallons of water.
  - They have the advantage of: being easily stored until needed, hold large volumes of water, cost effective at around $25, and remain in a bathtub minimizing the amount of space required. The disadvantage is that you have to fill the bladder before a SHTF event or before water becomes unavailable
- outside rain barrels to capture runoff water. Assumes you have rain.
- 2 liter soda bottles. A cheap and effective way to store emergency water.
  - You can store water in milk jugs but do not use it for drinking. This water should only be used for things like bathing, washing clothes, or other similar tasks.

- 5 gallon stackable water containers. A great option but slightly pricier.
- Water pouches such as those by Datrex.
- Washer
  - Many people don't consider this option but a washer is meant to hold and retain gallons of water without leaking. This makes it a great water storage vessel.

If times get desperate you can find water in the following locations:

- water heater

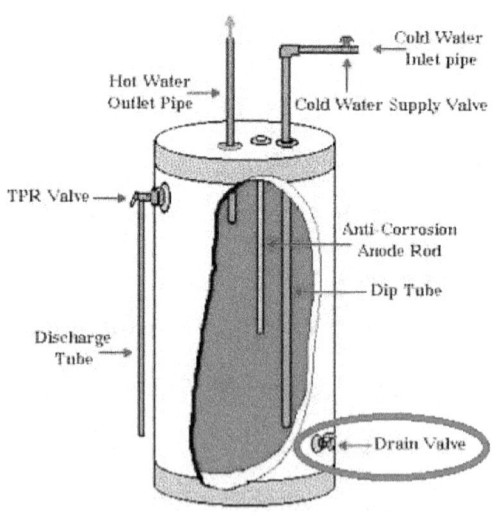

- water pipes throughout the house
- canned foods such as fruits and vegetables
- fire hydrants
- snow if available
- surface water, such as lakes and rivers
- neighbors

Last resort options include:

- toilet water stored in the cistern
  - Even though a toilet will provide about one to six gallons of water, including what's in the tank or cistern, it contains microorganisms as well as cleaning chemicals. Toilet water must be brought to a rolling boil or treated with chemicals
- Water beds
  - Waterbeds contain a significant amount of stagnant water and a haven for microorganisms.
- Swimming pools and/or hot tubs
- Fish tank

Once again these are last resort options that require proper purification before use. This list should begin to get you thinking about what options are available to you.

Remember to store water in a cool, dark area and replace every six to twelve months. If water storage containers/bottles are not marked with an expiration date, label each one with the current date and replace the water at least once per year.

If you have doubts about the quality of the water, boil it for a minimum of two minutes or chemically treat it. Examples of chemical treatment include:

- Calcium hypochlorite

  Also called pool shock or HTH (high-test hypochlorite), this chemical is often used in swimming pools. Make sure you purchase "pure" calcium hypochlorite (65 to 70 percent grade) that contains no other chemicals (e.g., clarifiers, anti-fungals, etc.). Follow the guidelines from the U.S. Army Center for Health Promotion and Preventive Medicine to make a diluted solution of calcium hypochlorite. You will add this solution to your main water supply to disinfect it. Do not drink the solution itself.

- o Place one heaping tablespoon of calcium hypochlorite in two gallons of water and wait for it to dissolve. Label this container "Calcium Hypochlorite Concentrate. DO NOT DRINK" and include the date you made it.
- o Once it's dissolved, add the concentrated solution you just made to your main supply of water to disinfect it. The suggested ratio is one part chlorine solution to one hundred parts water. This is equivalent to one pint of solution for every twelve and a half gallons of water (eight pints equals' one gallon).
- o Store any remaining calcium hypochlorite material (i.e., what's left in the package) in a cool, dry place and label appropriately.
- Chlorine bleach

This is a cheap and effective means of purifying water. Do not use scented bleaches, color-safe bleaches, or bleaches with added cleaners. Water treated with bleach, on average, will keep for approximatley six to twelve months.

The Washington State Department of Health (Health, 2009) has created the following guidelines:

Treating Water with a 5-6 Percent Liquid Chlorine Bleach Solution		
Volume of Water to be Treated	Treating Clear/Cloudy Water: Bleach Solution to Add	Treating Cloudy, Very Cold, or Surface Water: Bleach Solution to Add
1 quart/1 liter	3 drops	5 drops
1/2 gallon/2 quarts/2 liters	5 drops	10 drops
1 gallon	1/8 teaspoon (approximately 10 drops)	1/4 teaspoon
5 gallons	1/2 teaspoon	1 teaspoon
10 gallons	1 teaspoon	2 teaspoons

Wait one hour before drinking water treated with chlorine bleach. If there is a bleach taste or odor pour the water to be used back and forth between two pitchers or pans a couple of times. This will diminish the bleach odor.

Warning: Bleach can be extremely poisonous to the human body if not used properly and in the right amounts.

- Potassium permanganate

  This is another cheap and easy way to purify water. Potassium permanganate crystals can be bought at hardware stores.

  o Add three or four crystals per quart of water (or until the water stains a light pink) and let the water sit for thirty minutes.

Water treated with potassium permanganate can also be used as a disinfectant for cleaning wounds. Simply add crystals one by one until the water turns pink. You need a solution of approximately 0.01 percent, which requires about three or four crystals per quart of water.

- Purification tablets
  - These typically contain either iodine or chlorine and should be used according to the manufacturer's instructions.

- Tincture of iodine (2 percent)

Iodine is very effective against bacteria, viruses, and protozoa with the exception of cryptosporidium. When using iodine you must remember that the colder the water the longer it takes to disinfect. Most importantly, iodine is to be used on a short-term basis only. Iodine can be poisonous to humans, especially to young children. In addition you should be aware that iodine has a terrible taste. This is one of my least favorite methods of water purification.

  - If the water is mostly clear, use four drops of iodine per quart of water (sixteen drops of iodine per gallon).
  - If the water is cloudy, and you were unable to filter the water, use eight drops of iodine per quart (thirty-two drops per gallon).

- o Wait one hour before drinking water treated with tincture of iodine.

WARNING: Pregnant, nursing women or anyone with a thyroid condition should not use this method.

Non-chemical means of water purification include:

- Distillation. A process that utilizes a stove, large cooking pot, cooking pot lid, and a cup to capture purified water in the form of steam.
- Filtration units such as the Berkey™, the AquaRain™ Natural Water Filter, and the MSR Autoflow™ Gravity Water Filter.
- Hand-pump filters such as the MiniWorks EX™ Hand Pump Filter and the Katadyn™ Mini Ultralight Water Filter.
- Microfiltration water filters. These remove contaminants by passing water through a membrane. An example is the Katadyn™ Pocket filter.
- Survival straws. These use a highly efficient water purification system to destroy the

harmful bacteria and viruses that exist in most sources of water.

Food

On average, a person can go three weeks without food. Factors that will have a direct impact on how long you can go without food include the following:

- your health,
- your metabolism,
- your ratio of body fat to muscle,
- your hydration level,
- the temperature of your environment, and
- the work you are performing.

As with every element of The Survival Triangle© you must have food already stored before you have to shelter-in-place. There are two types of food supplies: short-term and long-term. Short-term foods supplies typically last three days to six months and are high in protein and calories whereas the purpose of long-term food supplies is to feed you and your family beyond six months, with one year being the goal. Short-term food supplies are the most appropriate for those who want to prepare to shelter-in-place. The amount of short term food you store will be based on your diet, weight, health, and number of people to feed. You will have to determine the amount (pounds) and types of food that are appropriate to you, your family, or group. There is no magic formula for amount of food to store but there are food storage serving matrixes that can be used as guidelines. For example, one food storage serving matrix recommends that four hundred pounds of wheat be stored per person which provides one year of servings. When determining how much food to store you need to consider how many calories per day you need to maintain your health and strength. In general most adults need between 1500 – 3000 calories per day. Here are several ideas on where to start:

- Grains - These typically store well for ten years, but wheat can last up to twenty years if stored properly. Grains include wheat berries, quinoa, oats, barley, flaxseed, and millet.
- Dried legumes (e.g., soybeans, split peas, and lentils) - Properly stored, these can last for seven to ten years.
- Dried fruits and vegetables - These can be kept for seven to ten years if properly stored.
- Rice - Properly stored, rice can be kept for seven to ten years.

- Corn - According to the Federal Emergency Management Administration, (FEMA), dried corn can be stored indefinitely, provided that it is properly stored in appropriate containers and isn't contaminated by insects, moisture, or other environmental contaminants.
- Honey - never spoils.
- Dry milk - This will last up to five years if stored properly.

Other foods to consider include the following:

- MREs (Meals-Ready-to-Eat) - A MRE is a self-contained, individual field ration in lightweight packaging that the United States military provides for its service members. MREs were designed for use in combat or other field conditions where organized food facilities are not available.
- Freeze-dried foods - These can be stored for up to twenty-five years in proper storage conditions.
- Dehydrated foods - a process of food preservation that works by removing water from the food, which inhibits the growth of microorganisms. Examples include iodized salt, white flour, cracked

wheat cereal, quick oats, rolled oats, buttermilk powder, and peanut butter powder.

- Comfort foods such as candy, canned soups, cookies, spaghetti, hamburgers, hot dogs, corn on the cob, chili, and ice cream.
- Fats and Oils

When storing food, don't forget items like spices, salt, pepper, vinegar, bouillon cubes, sugar, vegetable oil, shortening, baking powder, baking soda, yeast, and dry soup mixes. These items will help to give your food more flavors and make unfamiliar foods more appealing.

Food storage Shelf Life

Food storage is absolutely critical to maintain the nutrients and life of your foods. There are many food preservation options to select from including canning, dehydrating, freeze drying and the use of a multi-barrier system such as mylar. Once you've determined the most effective way to store your food it's critical to understand shelf life.

As Joan Crain (Crain, 2007) explains:

"The question frequently asked is, "What is the shelf life of my food storage?" First, let's define "food storage" and "shelf life".

- Food storage generally refers to long term foods that are low in moisture and can be stored for a long time.
- Shelf life is defined in two ways:
  - "best if used by" – the length of time foods are best in taste and nutrition. (See more on this type of food storage shelf life here.)
  - "life sustaining" food shelf life – the length of time foods can be stored and still edible.

There can be a big time difference between these two types of food products. Foods bought at the grocery store can have a shelf life of a few days to several years, depending on the type of food, the storage conditions, and the packaging. That's why those products have a "best if used by" date which is required by law.

The "life sustaining" foods are those that are packaged specifically for long term storage. The estimated shelf life for many of these products has increased to 30 years or more (see chart below).

If stored more than 30 years, taste and nutritional quality will decline, depending on the quality of the food when first packaged. However, studies have shown that these foods, even if stored past their designated time, retain their calories and calories will sustain life in an emergency and prevent starvation.

Food storage shelf life for long term food storage depends on 4 main criteria:

- Temperature
- Moisture
- Oxygen
- Light

Let's look at these one at a time.

<u>Temperature</u>

Foods stored at room temperature or cooler (75°F/24°C or lower) will be nutritious and edible much longer than previously thought according to findings of recent scientific studies. Foods stored at 50°F to 60°F (which is optimal) will last longer than foods stored at higher temperatures. Heat absolutely destroys food and its nutritional value. Proteins break down and some vitamins will be destroyed. Taste, color, and smell of some foods may also change.

Moisture

The reason long term food storage is dehydrated or freeze dried is to eliminate moisture. Too much moisture promotes an atmosphere where microorganisms can grow and chemical reaction in foods causing deterioration that ultimately can sicken us.

Oxygen

Too much oxygen can deteriorate foods and promote the growth of microorganisms, especially in fats, vitamins, and food colors. That is the reason to use oxygen absorbers when dry packing your own food products.

Light

Exposure to too much light can cause deterioration of foods. In particular it affects food colors, vitamin loss, fats and oils, and proteins. Keep long term food storage in low light areas for longest shelf life.

Long Term Food Shelf Life Chart

(The years listed for shelf life assumes ideal storage conditions, i.e. low moisture, low light, cool temperatures, and low oxygen content.)

See the following two pages for Long Term Food Shelf Life Charts

Food	"Life Sustaining" Shelf-Life Estimates (In Years)
Apple slices	30
Alfalfa Seeds	8
Bakers Flour	15
Barley	10
Black Turtle Beans	15 - 20
Blackeye Peas	15 -20
Buckwheat	15
Butter/margarine Powder	15
Cocoa Powder	15
Cornmeal	5
Cracked wheat	25
Durham Wheat	8-12
Flax	8-12
Flour (white)	10-20
Flour (whole wheat)	10-20
Garbanzo Beans	15 - 20
Garden Seeds	4
Gluten	5
Granola	5
Honey, Salt and Sugar	Indefinitely
Hulled Oats	30
Kidney Beans	20
Lentils	20
Lima Beans	20
Millet	8-12
Morning Moo	10

Food	"Life Sustaining" Shelf-Life Estimates (In Years)
Onions	8-12
Pasta	30
Pearled Oats	10
Pink Beans	20 - 30
Pinto Beans	30+
Potatoes (flakes, slices, diced)	30
Powdered Eggs	15
Powdered Milk	20
Quinoa	8
Rice (brown)	6 months
Rice (white)	25+
Rolled Oats	30
Rye	8
Small Red Beans	8-10
Soy Beans	8-10
Special bakery wheat	25
Spelt	12
Sprouting Seeds	4-5
Triticale	8-12
TVP	15 - 20
Unbleached Flour	5
Vegetables (most)	20-30
Wheat (hard white)	30
Wheat (hard red)	30+
Wheat flakes	5
Whey Powder	15
Yeast	2

(Crain, 2007)

<u>Shelter</u>

When you shelter-in-place you need to ensure you prepare your shelter for multiple types of events. Examples of events that you may want to prepare for include tornado, hurricane, chemical/nuclear release, pandemic (avian bird flu), drought conditions, wildfire, terrorism (9/11 – Boston Marathon incident), economic collapse, and temporary loss of the power grid (electricity, water, sewer). Each event will have similar Survival Triangle© elements such as food, water, and heat, but because each event is unique there needs to be different considerations. For example, living close to a nuclear power plant may require you to purchase iodine tablets or a nuclear/biological/chemical (NBC) suit. A side note, if you live or work within 10 miles of a nuclear power plant, states will provide iodine tablets at no cost. Living in a hurricane area will require that you have boards pre-cut for windows and doors. Living next to a fertilizer plant may require that you have a gas mask to protect against ammonium nitrate. Ammonium nitrate is an explosive chemical produced by fertilizer plants that can cause life threatening injuries when ignited. The following is a list of recommendations you may have to take or prepare prior to sheltering-in-place:

- Close all window shades, blinds, or curtains
- Close and lock all doors
- Keep sheets of pre-cut plastic which can be taped around the doors, windows, and heating ventilation and air conditioning (HVAC) units to limit circulation in your shelter.
  - As an additive measure use duct tape around all door, window, and HVAC openings
- Create a checklist outlining procedures that should take place once you have sheltered-in-place.
- Pre-cut boards to fit window and door frames

Heat

If you live in the Northern, Midwestern, or Eastern portion of the United States, heat is essential. Without heat, pipes freeze, water freezes, hypothermia sets in, and your life becomes extremely miserable. Heat sources can be fixed or portable. Fixed heat sources can include wood stoves, propane tanks, natural gas heaters, geothermal, and electric sources. Examples of portable heat sources include the Yukon M1950, the Big Buddy™, and kerosene heaters.

In many shelter-in-place scenarios, electricity may be a luxury. This is obviously a problem if your house's primary source of heat is electrical. For example, if you have natural gas you can continue to generate heat for your shelter, but your fan or blower won't circulate that heat without electricity. Thus, you need to have multiple backup sources of fuel for heat. Backup fuel sources include resources such as wood, kerosene, home heating fuel, propane, diesel, and even jet fuel. Below I've listed several of my backup heat sources and fuels should I have to shelter-in-place. In addition I explain why I chose them.

Take, for instance, the Yukon M1950 stove. U.S. soldiers in the Korean War used this stove, and it can now be purchased in military-surplus stores for approximately $170. It is extremely compact when not in use, yet it assembles to provide a fully functional source of heat. This stove can use many types of fuel, including wood, jet fuel, diesel fuel, and unleaded gasoline. The entire unit weighs only twenty-eight pounds. I can easily pick it up and carry it anywhere, or use it in the house if I need to. It is perfect for both sheltering-in-place and bugging out.

Yukon M- 1950

The Big Buddy™ is a good example of a propane heat source that can further your redundancy. Mr. Heater's Big Buddy™ can use propane cylinders in a variety of sizes, from the one-pound cylinders you can buy at Walmart™ or Target™. The Big Buddy™ can also accommodate larger twenty-pound cylinders. The propane cylinders connect on each side of the Big Buddy™ (inside the door) and provide ample heating times.

I've used the Big Buddy™ for some time now, and I like the compactness as well as the BTUs. The Big Buddy™

has a built-in blower that can circulate heated air for heating efficiency when used indoors. The fan operates on either four D-size batteries or a six-volt A/C adapter. From a safety perspective, the Big Buddy™ has a low-oxygen shut-off system, tip-over shut-off system, and a heavy-duty safety guard.

A third form of heating redundancy that I use is a kerosene heater. There are two types of kerosene heaters: convection and radiant. Both types have circular fiberglass wicks that use capillary action to transport the kerosene straight to the burner. In a radiant kerosene heater, the burner is in a glass cylinder that has repellent stainless steel behind it. When you turn on the device, the burner turns red and sends heat waves outward. Radiant kerosene heaters produce some convection heat, but they mostly project the heat forward, to the walls and windows. Convection is simply the movement of the air around the kerosene heater due to a temperature increase. Kerosene can last up to five years if properly stored in approved metal or plastic containers. K-1 kerosene is safe because it burns cleanly, and if you have the wick set properly, it gives off little or no smoke. The kerosene heater is economical in terms of fuel cost. In the Midwest, kerosene heaters runs anywhere from fifty dollars to two hundred dollars.

Remember that heat is the result of fire. In addition to keeping you warm, fire can also provide light and allows you to cook food. If there were no electricity, and I had to shelter-in-place, my kerosene heater would provide light and heat. It would also serve as a stove top. To cook I would simply place my cooking container on top of the wire cage surrounding the kerosene heater. Point is that any time you have to shelter-in-place you need to be creative with the resources you have available.

Self-Preservation: Protection

Once again let's go back to The Survival Triangle©. As described earlier, self-preservation is comprised of two components: mental and physical requirements. An extremely important physical requirement is security or protection. Without protection, assuming you had to shelter-in-place for an extended period of time, your food, water, heat, and shelter are in jeopardy. The reason is simple. People will react differently in a significant life-altering event. First and foremost people will always look out for themselves and their families. More to the point, people will not act as they did prior to the event, and this will include the relationships they had with other peers, families, groups, and so on. If you have to shelter-in-place for extended periods of time, say two weeks, neighbors and friends will probably run out of food and water due to a lack of preparation. They will do whatever they can to find these resources, obtaining it by any means within their power — up to and including violence. Be ready to protect yourself and family. My preparations include food for others outside of my family. Once that food is gone, there is no more. The remaining food will only be made available to my immediate family.

When the word protection is mentioned, the first thing that comes to mind is firearms. As we all know, firearms come in various sizes, models, prices, types, and yes, they are necessary. As you prepare to shelter-in-place I recommend the purchase of several shotguns; two at a minimum. Shotguns give you the widest shot pattern and target area for close quarter confrontations. In addition, the cost of a shotgun is significantly cheaper than rifles and handguns and the ammunition is much more available. I have several shotguns and to keep ammunition cost down I buy the 100 round value packs at Walmart™ for around $25. As you decide which brand of shotgun to purchase I would suggest you purchase two of the same model. This is for several reasons. First, the operation of each shotgun will be the same. Second, each shotgun will use the same ammunition and therefore not require different caliber types. And third, the parts from one shotgun can be used to repair the other. Because this subject is both controversial and personal I will leave it to you, the reader, to determine the best option(s).

Other Considerations

<u>Medical Supplies</u>

Although they are not specifically mentioned in The Survival Triangle©, medical knowledge and supplies are critical when sheltering-in-place. Obtaining medical knowledge could be as simple as taking a CPR or first-aid course, or arranging for access to a medically knowledgeable resource such as EMTs, nurses, physician assistants, or even doctors. Medical resources also include books and guides that explain how to deal with specific circumstances in an emergency. In addition, it's important to have the proper basic medical supplies on hand. There may be many medical concerns while sheltering-in-place but you won't be able to cover them all. Being prepared for the basics will help. Always have an Emergency Bug-out Bag (EBOB). This is not to be confused with a Bug-out Bag (BOB), which contains personal items such as clothes, bug-out gear, and so on. An EBOB will contain emergency supplies and resources, see list below, which will be useful should an emergency situation arise. An EBOB should contain at least one to two months' supply of any medication you're taking. If you have to shelter-in-place for multiple weeks it may become extremely difficult to get refills or new prescriptions. For example, my son is asthmatic and as such we have at least two months' supply of inhalers on hand at any one time.

Basic medical supplies should give you the capability to treat minor to serious issues. Given the vast array of medical possibilities, you're not going to be able to store everything. Store the essentials, which include but are no means limited to the following:

- Abdominal/pressure pad
- Ace bandages
- Adhesive bandages (assorted sizes and types)
- Alcohol (both 50 percent and 91 percent by volume)
- Alcohol wipes/antiseptic
- Antibiotic ointment (stock up on this)
- Betadine
- Burn Gel (a 2 percent lidocaine-based salve)
- Celox (stops bleeding in as little as thirty seconds)
- Gauze (assorted sizes and types)
- Hydrogen peroxide

- Ibuprofen/acetaminophen/Imodium/Benadryl/ Zyrtec or similar drugs
- Instant cold/hot Packs
- Iodine wipes and/or swabs
- Liquid Skin or similar substance
- NIOSH-certified N95 Mask (filters out H1N1)
- Personal medications
- Printed material (books, pamphlets, guides, etc.)
- Splinter-removal kit
- Sting-relief wipes
- Super glue
- Tape, scissors, latex gloves, tweezers, and thermometer
- Tourniquet
- Wound-care kit with various sutures

Communication Media

When sheltering-in-place you should have multiple communication platforms available. These will keep you informed of the current conditions and future plans. These tools will help determine when it's no longer necessary to shelter-in-place and if any additional actions should be taken. Below are examples of some useful communication devices and their characteristics:

- Emergency dynamo radio - This is a great radio to have as many brands can operate from a battery, electricity, or dynamo. When batteries or electricity are not available, the radio works via the dynamo. The dynamo is charged by cranking a handle in circular motions which charges an internal battery.
- Shortwave radios - Shortwave radios can receive radio transmissions on frequencies between three and thirty MHz, which enables worldwide communications and the ability to stay informed. In addition, shortwave radios can be heard from thousands of miles away and are extremely economical to purchase. Shortwave radios can operate off of a 12 volt car battery.
- Cell phones – a great, portable option. However, there have been many events in which cell phones have been useless. During 9/11 cellular service requirements were so overwhelming that very few calls were completed.

- Land lines – an alternative to a cell phone. There are times when a land line is available and cell phones aren't.
- Internet – assuming it's available
- MURS (Multi-Use Radio Service) - MURS are two-way radios with a limited transmitter-power output of two watts. The radios are capable of transmitting three to four miles based on line-of-sight, and one to two miles with minimal blockage from buildings or trees. MURS are economical to purchase and practical, as they transmit and receive on frequencies relatively unknown to the general population. MURS are battery operated.
- CB radios (Citizen Band radios) - CB radios can transmit no farther than 155 miles per FCC regulations, but in practice, they transmit no more than four to twenty miles based on line-of-sight. They are economical to purchase and would be a great addition when sheltering-in-place. Operates off of a 12 volt battery
- GMRS (General Mobile Radio Service) - GMRS radios require a valid GMRS license to operate. They are FM/UHF radios that operate at short

distances only. They are moderately priced. GMRS radios are battery operated.

- Ham radio (amateur radio) - Ham radios require a license and transmit on frequency modulation (FM) and single sideband (SSB). Ham radios receive and transmit throughout the world and are moderately to high priced. Ham radios are highly recommended when sheltering-in-place as they have the ability to operate from a 12 volt battery.
- Television – assuming electricity is available.

<u>Lighting</u>

The focus of this section will be portable lighting as required when sheltering-in-place. Portable lighting is used whenever your primary light sources are not available. For example, in a rainstorm the power goes out, and you need light. One would typically light an oil lamp or bring out the flashlights. These are examples of portable lighting in that they are easily accessible and lightweight. Furthermore, they produce sufficient lumens (a measure of the total "amount" of visible light emitted by a source), and they can travel with you wherever you need to go. Below are examples of lighting options and their characteristics. Examples include:

- Flashlights, headlamps, lanterns, and fluorescent strips - The majority use standard batteries. The cost is relatively inexpensive, dependent on brand, and they can provide redundant lighting sources for family members (i.e., more than one light source). These types of lights vary in lumens and weight for portability. Standardize on one type of battery for all your flashlights. For example, I highly recommend AAA-size batteries as they can be used in flashlights and headlamps.

- Outdoor solar lights - Solar lights are recharged by the sun via a solar panel. They have several advantages, such as using a renewable energy source (i.e., the sun) and can be easily found at any local hardware store. In addition to being portable they are inexpensive, ranging from four dollars to sixty dollars. Simply bring them indoor's at night when you need light and set them out during the day to recharge.

- Light sticks - Light sticks are easy to store and use. They have a short life span of one to sixteen hours.

If you chose to purchase light sticks, I recommend buying in small bulk units on eBay, Amazon, or other sources. I prefer the yellow-colored light sticks.

- Candles - I highly recommend honey candles over wax perfumed candles. Candles are portable but do present a fire hazard due to the open flame.
- Dynamo flashlights/lanterns - Dynamo flashlight/lanterns use the Faraday principle of electromagnetic energy to eliminate the need for batteries. Basically, by cranking a handle, energy is created and then stored in rechargeable battery cells. This stored energy is used to power the bulb. As the flashlight is used it has to be recharged (cranked) to provide sufficient lighting.
- Kerosene lamps - Kerosene lamps come in many forms including Aladdin Lamps. The amount of heat, which directly impacts how much light is produced, is adjusted by a wick. They are easily transported from location to location but do present a fire hazard if tipped over.
- White-fuel lanterns - White-fuel lanterns are available from many manufacturers, with the most

recognizable being Coleman™. The fuel is easily purchased at local retailers, and I would highly recommend buying extra mantels, glass globes, and pumps. White-fuel lanterns are portable and reasonably priced, but they are a fire hazard if used inappropriately.

- LEDs (Light Emitting Diodes) - LEDs come in various types, from large lanterns to those worn on your head or body. LEDs can operate on everything from twelve-volt battery banks to AAA-size batteries. Most portable LEDs worn on the head or body operate off of AAA-size or AA-size batteries.

- Propane lanterns - Typical propane lanterns use one-pound propane cylinders, which are sold at local retailers (e.g., Target™, Walmart™, etc.). They are easy to use, convenient, portable, and cost effective. Once again they pose a fire hazard if used inappropriately.

- Oil lamps - Oil lamps operate off of lamp oil (i.e., liquid petroleum). The amount of light desired is adjusted by raising the wick up or down. Oil lamps are both portable and cost-effective. They pose a fire hazard if used inappropriately.

- Aladdin lamps – similar to oil lamps but use kerosene as the fuel source. Aladdin lamps are considerably brighter than oil lamps.

Basic Sheltering-in-place guidelines

If a SHTF situation occurs, there will be a timeframe where you shelter-in-place, dependent on the magnitude and effects of the event. This is why you need to be prepared. The timeframe will vary based on the type of event/scenario, your provisions, the severity of the situation, your comfort level, the availability of a vehicle or bug out location, time of the year, and so on.

Sheltering-in-place not only provides security it also allows for the emotions of the event to be processed and hopefully better understood. During the Boston Marathon domestic terrorism incident, city officials mandated that citizen's shelter-in-place. This was for two reasons as I see it: security and emotions. Because the location of the two suspects were unknown, it was critical that officials ensure the safety of all Bostonians. This could only happen by sheltering-in-place. The mandate to shelter-in-place allowed law enforcement officials to more easily collect evidence and search for the suspected terrorist. From an emotional perspective, when the incident first occurred, information was scarce and unreliable. Emotions were extremely high as runners and bystanders were wounded and/or treating those who were wounded. Tension was high. The entire city was looking for answers and direction. By sheltering-in-place individuals and families were allowed to reflect on what had happened and await further communication; all in a secure environment.

During the initial stage of any SHTF situation that requires sheltering-in-place, there will be confusion, lack of direction, chaos, and many unanswered questions. The population will be looking for guidance on what steps to take next, as well as information about the situation (i.e., what caused it, how long it will continue, when the electricity will be on, where to find first-aid stations, how to get food, etc.). All levels of government — local, county, state, and federal — will be extremely selective about when, how, and what they communicate. When you shelter-in-place, you do not expose yourself or your loved ones to the chaos (i.e., to either the chaotic situation or other people who are not prepared).

Within hours, and sometimes days, of the situation, the landscape will change dramatically. Individuals and families who aren't properly prepared will begin to panic.

They will begin to realize that if assistance hasn't arrived, it most likely isn't going to arrive any time soon. Their limited food and supplies will have been consumed, and the grocery and hardware stores will have nothing else available. The biggest concern will be the lack of food and water. These individuals will begin to look outside their usual sources and ask others for basic supplies. Maybe others will give, but maybe they won't. As time goes by, people will become even more desperate. In order to protect their loved ones and save their lives, they may do things they would never have done previously. When this stage arrives, and preferably some time before, head to your bug-out location should you have one. If you have no bug out location or are unable to reach it, you will continue to shelter-in-place while always remaining vigilant.

Where you shelter-in-place or bug out to must provide you and your family the necessities of life, but remember, it won't remove the challenges that remain ahead. How well you prepared will determine the actions you take and how long you will be able to shelter-in-place.

Redundancy

As you prepare items that will be necessary to shelter-in-place, make sure you understand the concept of redundancy. Redundancy means making sure you have alternative or multiple capabilities for each corner of The Survival Triangle©. In a previous example I used heat and the multiple forms I have available. The point is that if one source fails, you should have multiple backup technologies, albeit some simple, to solve the problem. Another example of redundancy is food types. You should have multiple types of food ranging from freeze dried, dehydrated, canned, to Mylar packed. I think you understand the point.

How long to Shelter-in-Place

You shelter-in-place as long as it takes for the event, or the effects of the event, to be rendered safe. This is often a personal judgment call but can be aided by information from various sources. Sources can include: neighbors, newspapers, television, short wave radio, local/county/state/federal governments, and the internet. At times government authorities will directly indicate that it's no longer necessary to shelter-in-place.

My family is prepared to shelter-in-place for approximately six months. We're not preparing for a TEOTWAWKI (The End of the World As We Know It) situation. Instead, we're focused on an event such as a tornado, earthquake, hurricane, flood, economic crisis, or short term man-made events — basically anything that would have a mass effect on society with severe repercussions. In most instances, six months should be more than enough time for electricity, food, water, and other essential services to be restored.

In conclusion, I would state that we're all aware that there is no guarantee in life, let alone in the decisions we make. But what I do know is that being properly prepared to shelter-in-place can negate a negative outcome in many situations. In order to properly shelter-in-place you must do so from a balanced perspective as modeled by The Survival Triangle©.

Sheltering-in-place is one scenario that a group known as preppers plan for. Should you have an interest in preppers or prepping and would like detailed information see my other books which are available at Amazon.com. They are: The Prepper's Survival Guide: An

Introduction to Prepping and a Guide to Fire, The Prepper's Handbook, and The Christian Prepper's Handbook; all listed under the author name "Zion Prepper".

I hope you found the information in The Prepper's Survival Guide Series: A Guide to Sheltering-in-Place valuable and God bless the United States of America.

Bibliography

Army, U. (n.d.). Emergency Drinking Water Disinfection Procedure. Retrieved October 6, 2011, from Emergency Drinking Water Disinfection Procedure: phc.amedd.army.mil/PHC%20Resource%20Library/31-008-1004.pdf

Blaney, B. (2013, February 25). 2nd blizzard in less than week slams Plains region. Retrieved April 28, 2013, from news.yahoo.com: http://news.yahoo.com/2nd-blizzard-less-week-slams-plains-region-124708575.html

Crain, J. (2007). Food Storage Shelf Life. Retrieved May 9, 2013, from Family Survival Planning: http://www.family-survival-planning.com/long-term-food-shelf-life.html

Health, W. S. (2009, January). Public Health and Response. Retrieved October 6, 2011, from Purifying Household Water: http://www.doh.wa.gov/phepr/handbook/purify.htm

Joe Sutton, D. A. (2013, February 12). Cruise ship still gross, passengers say, but it's finally moving. Retrieved

April 28, 2013, from CNN.com:
http://www.cnn.com/2013/02/12/travel/cruise-ship-fire

Lindsay, J. (2013, February 9). Huge storm blankets Northeast with 2 feet of snow. Retrieved April 28, 2013, from Yahoo News: http://news.yahoo.com/huge-storm-blankets-northeast-2-142830361.html

Mullen, J. (2013, April 1). 2 dead in China from unusual bird flu strain. Retrieved April 28, 2013, from CNN.com: http://www.cnn.com/2013/04/01/world/asia/china-bird-flu-deaths

Naylor, B. (2013, April 22). Boston Lockdown 'Extraordinary' But Prudent, Experts Say. Retrieved April 27, 2013, from National Public Radio (NPR): http://www.npr.org/2013/04/22/178446136/boston-lockdown-extraordinary-but-prudent-experts-say

Stableford, D. (2013, April 7). Is North Korea on the brink of war? Retrieved April 28, 2013, from news.yahoo.com: http://news.yahoo.com/blogs/lookout/north-korea-kim-jong-un-war-201715650.html